Beetle
Wants To Fly

by Jackie Walter and Elisa Patrissi

FRANKLIN WATTS
LONDON•SYDNEY

Beetle lived in a big green field.

She liked to walk in the leaves.

She liked to climb up
the tall grass.
Beetle was happy in the field.

3

One day, Beetle was walking in the leaves. Ladybird saw Beetle walking and started to laugh.

"Why are you walking?" asked Ladybird. "Why don't you fly?"

"I can't fly," said Beetle.

"Flying is better," said Ladybird.
And away she went.

Beetle was sad.
She wanted to fly, too.

The next day, Beetle climbed up
the tall grass.
She looked down.

She saw some baby birds
in a nest.

"Oh!" said Beetle.

She was so surprised to see the baby birds that she fell off the grass and into the nest.

11

Beetle did not want the baby birds to see her.

"They will eat me," she said.

"I cannot walk away. I must hide."

Soon, Mother Bird came to feed the baby birds.

Beetle climbed up on
Mother Bird's back.

Soon all the food was gone.
Mother Bird had to go and
get some more food for
the baby birds.

Up, up, up went Mother Bird.
Beetle held on to
Mother Bird's back.

Beetle saw Ladybird flying by.

"Help!" cried Beetle.

"I don't like flying!"

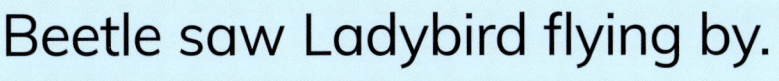

When Mother Bird got back
to the nest, Beetle jumped down
onto the grass.

"I don't like flying," said Beetle.

"Walking is better for me!"

Story trail

Start

Start at the beginning of the story trail. Ask your child to retell the story in their own words, pointing to each picture in turn to recall the sequence of events.

Independent Reading

This series is designed to provide an opportunity for your child to read on their own. These notes are written for you to help your child choose a book and to read it independently.

In school, your child's teacher will often be using reading books which have been banded to support the process of learning to read. Use the book band colour your child is reading in school to help you make a good choice. *Beetle Wants to Fly* is a good choice for children reading at Green Band in their classroom to read independently. The aim of independent reading is to read this book with ease, so that your child enjoys the story and relates it to their own experiences.

About the book
Beetle meets Ladybird and wants to fly too. But after climbing too high and falling on to a bird's back, Beetle decides it is much safer being on the ground.

Before reading
Help your child to learn how to make good choices by asking: "Why did you choose this book? Why do you think you will enjoy it?" Look at the cover together and ask: "What do you think the story will be about?" Support your child to think of what they already know about the story context. Read the title aloud and ask: "What creatures can you see on the cover? What are the differences between them?" Remind your child that they can try to sound out the letters to make a word if they get stuck.

Decide together whether your child will read the story independently or read it aloud to you. When books are short, as at Green Band, your child may wish to do both!

During reading

If reading aloud, support your child if they hesitate or ask for help by telling the word. Remind your child of what they know and what they can do independently. If reading to themselves, remind your child that they can come and ask for your help if stuck.

After reading

Support comprehension by asking your child to tell you about the story. Use the story trail to encourage your child to retell the storyin the right sequence, in their own words.

Give your child a chance to respond to the story: "Did you have a favourite part? Why did Beetle want to fly?"

Help your child think about the messages in the book that go beyond the story and ask: "How does Beetle feel at the end of the story? What does Beetle learn? How would you describe Ladybird's behaviour?"

Extending learning

Help your child understand the story structure by using the same story context and adding different elements. "Let's make up a new story about a creature that wants to swim across water. Which creature would you choose? What happens in your story?"

In the classroom, your child's teacher may be reinforcing punctuation and how it informs the way we group words in sentences. On a few of the pages, ask your child to find the speech marks that show us where someone is talking and then read it aloud, making it sound like talking. Find the question marks and ask your child to practise the expression they used for asking questions.

Franklin Watts
First published in Great Britain in 2023
by Hodder and Stoughton
Copyright © Hodder and Stoughton, 2023

Series Editors: Jackie Hamley and Melanie Palmer
Series Advisors: Dr Sue Bodman and Glen Franklin
Series Designers: Cathryn Gilbert and Peter Scoulding

A CIP catalogue record for this book is
available from the British Library.

ISBN 978 1 4451 7424 2 (hbk)
ISBN 978 1 4451 7464 8 (pbk)
ISBN 978 1 4451 7482 2 (ebook)

Printed in China

Franklin Watts
An imprint of
Hachette Children's Group
Part of Hodder and Stoughton
Carmelite House
50 Victoria Embankment
London EC4Y 0DZ

An Hachette UK Company
www.hachette.co.uk

www.reading-champion.co.uk